COCKATIELS

THE ESSENTIAL GUIDE TO OWNERSHIP, CARE, & TRAINING FOR YOUR PET

Kate H. Pellham

© 2015

DISCLAIMER

This book is not intended as a substitute for the medical advice of a veterinarian. The reader should regularly consult a veterinarian in matters relating to his/her pet's health and particularly with respect to any symptoms that may require diagnosis or medical attention.

Photos copyright respective owners, licensed through stock sites unless otherwise noted.

Table of Contents

Introduction

Who can resist the adorable charm and sweet
disposition of cockatiels? Many of the endearing
qualities existing in other animals can be readily found
in a well handled "tiel". If you want a pet bird that will
happily perch on your shoulder, one who craves your

company and voice, a bird to have as a friend for years to come, then a cockatiel is for you.

Cockatiels that are allowed to live in the sort of environment where its highly sociable and inquisitive nature thrives make some of the best pets around. Their small size allows bird-lovers living in any home the chance to own a pet. Even a small studio apartment that is properly equipped can make a wonderful home for these birds.

If you're the type of pet owner who's looking for an intelligent creature that will require bonding time and return affection lovingly, then look no further than cockatiels. On the other hand, if you prefer a pet you can admire from afar but not have to interact with, then these birds aren't for you. Cockatiels have an innate desire to bond with others, to learn new things and to receive and give friendship.

This book will teach you everything you need to know to create a home that will make any cockatiel chirp happily. With patience and dedication, you can have a pet that seeks your company much like a puppy, enjoys being petted like a kitten, and is an unforgettable bird that will continually entertain you with its unique blend of playful antics.

Chapter 1: Cockatiels as Pets

Cockatiels make wonderful pets. These birds have delightful personalities and each cockatiel has its own unique set of traits, making these creatures far more interesting. Any cockatiel pet owner will tell you their feathered friend can rival the antics of other birds, including other species of parrots (Cockatiels are a type of parrot) and their cousin, the cockatoos. The charm and playful characteristics of "tiels" make them one of the most popular pet birds in the world.

These little heartbreakers are the second most popular pet bird around, second only to parakeets. With their adorable orange cheek patches, inquisitive and playful demeanor, it's easy to see why. A well-handled bird can greet you with kisses, perch on your shoulders as you watch TV or go about your daily tasks, and even come when called. Many cockatiels can mimic human words. These birds will typically act excited when they see their owners, much like a happy puppy would.

There's so much to love about these creatures. Owning one will add joy and laughter to your home, provided your own lifestyle and personality matches that of a good cockatiel pet owner.

Making an Important Decision

But is owning a pet cockatiel right for you? Just like no dog is the perfect match for any type of dog-lover (some are too energetic to live in an apartment, while other dogs don't have the right temperament for small children) not everyone has the lifestyle, time, preference and personality that match that of a responsible cockatiel handler.

Here are several key things you need to know about cockatiels to help you decide if you can provide the environment it needs to lead a healthy and happy life:

- **High energy level.** Cockatiels are, without a doubt, active birds. They require plenty of stimulation and may begin to exhibit destructive behavior—such as plucking their own feathers—when they get too bored. You, the owner, should have time each day to spend with your

14

cockatiel. Your activities together could be as simple as watching TV with the bird by your side, or spending some time each day reading aloud to your pet. Because cockatiels are high-energy pets, they require a spacious bird cage. The minimum recommended cage size should have a dimension of 24" x 24". Your bird will need bird toys and pet perches to keep it occupied and mentally stimulated.

- **Lengthy Lifespan.** Owning a pet cockatiel means making a commitment spanning over a decade or even more. When kept in captivity, these creatures can live for an average span of 15 to 20 years. Sometimes it can be as short as 12 years—still a long time to commit to a pet! There are reports of cockatiels who lived for 30 years and even longer.

- **Requires bonding and training.** Perhaps you're thinking of acquiring a pet cockatiel because you saw a friend's bird hop on a finger and give its owner kisses. Maybe your young child saw a tamed bird on TV and is now begging for one of his own. Keep in mind that cockatiels are intelligent creatures with unique personalities. Not all cockatiels behave alike. Also, don't expect to bring home a new pet cockatiel and have it act as sweet as a purring kitten off the bat. Earning the bird's trust will take time and patience. In most cases, you will have to put in hours and hours bonding with a cockatiel before it begins to behave affectionately. Some birds even react violently at first, especially in cases of older cockatiels who weren't taught to bond with humans at an early age.

- **They can bite.** Though it's not difficult with time and patience to tame a cockatiel and they're not known to be aggressive creatures, a cockatiel can bite and the bite may lead to minor and even severe injury. When these birds bite, they usually do so out of fear, not aggression. But since the danger of being bitten by a pet that possesses a sharp beak exists, it's not advisable for young children to own or handle cockatiels. Even the sweetest bird may react negatively from the tight grip of a small child who can't help but squeeze the cute bird.

- **Cage cleaning.** Just like all pet birds, cockatiels will leave droppings in their cage at all hours of the day. This means you, the pet owner, must have enough time each day cleaning its cage to keep your bird's living quarters germ-free. Cockatiels are also playful enough to toy with their food, spilling quite a few particles in the process. This means you'll have to clean up the cage pretty much the same way a parent would a toddler's eating area. Make sure you have the time and patience to keep your pet's cage clean each day since a filthy cage can easily cause any animal to get sick.

- **Sounds they emit.** Cockatiels aren't known to learn human words as quickly as some parrot species—there are exceptions, of course, since every bird is different—but they can still be noisy little housemates. These pets can screech, whistle or mimic our sounds. Only get a pet cockatiel if you're fine with a pet that makes a bit of noise. Don't worry, it's not as loud and bothersome as a yelping puppy. Unless you have a neighbor with ultra sensitive hearing, most cockatiels that are kept indoors won't be garnering you noise complaints.

Once you've taken these important points into consideration and you're convinced a pet cockatiel is right for you and your household, read on to discover more about these fascinating animals.

Origin and Background

Cockatiels are known to hail from all over Australia, except in the region of Tasmania. They prefer to live in the eastern parts of the country, choosing dry inlands over the coastal spots. The open environment provided by the Australian land mass is thought to be the reason why these birds don't possess the loud screeching sound of parrots, especially parrots that come from rain-forest environments. This bird was initially discovered in 1770, but it didn't become a popular pet before the Australian gold rush occurred around the early 20th century. The initial sightings of cockatiels were reported by folks who arrived in Australia along with Captain Cook.

Cockatiels were once called *Nymphicus* in the early 1800s and were later taken to England and the rest of Europe, thanks to prevalent expeditions occurring during that century. While certain differences have been noted in the geographical populations, there are no subspecies of cockatiels

Cockatiels in the wild search for food by flying close to the ground as they forage for their next meal. If you witness these birds in the wild, you may find them amongst a large flock of their own kind, circling the sky while looking for bodies of water. Lakes and the like offer cockatiels a place to breed, rest and seek refuge from the heat.

These birds have no trouble breeding in the wild and also breed with little difficulty in captivity, making them even more popular as pets. Their ease of breeding in captivity keeps the cost of purchasing a cockatiel fairly low.

In their natural habitat, cockatiels are frequently on high alert for predators. Because of this, they are light sleepers. It's not rare for a pet cockatiel to experience what's known as **night-fright**. A bird going through one of these episodes may thrash around its cage, acting very startled.

Tip: If you happen to have a pet cockatiel that experiences frequent night-frights, you can remedy the situation by leading it back to its perch stand and keeping a night light near the cage.

Appearance of Cockatiels

Cockatiel breeders over the years have found ways to breed them in unique colors. Today, these birds come in many lovely color mutations, owning more colorful feathers than their original counterparts from decades and centuries ago.

You can now choose cockatiels in a wide array of hues. Some have grey feathers while others are colored yellow, soft brown, white and silver. There are a few select breeders with green mutations.

Furthermore, the markings of these creatures also vary. Some cockatiels have markings on different body parts while others come in solid colors, such as an all-white variety, or those with solid pearl hues. Plenty of cockatiels are made extra adorable thanks to orange, yellow, white, peach or gray cheek patches.

You may find cockatiels with unique appearances, like the cinnamon pearl pied whitefaces. These birds have mostly white feathers, plus a light cocoa brown shade around their wings. They may also have patches on their bodies. Some of these patches may appear in a lace-like pattern known as pearl markings. Female cockatiels that appear this way typically have light brown cheek patches while their male counterparts usually have all-white faces and no cheek patches.

Cockatiels possess an average length of approximately 14 inches and usually weigh anywhere from 75 to 120 grams, although it's not unusual for some well-fed pets to weigh as much as 200 grams.

All about the Personality

Sociable Creatures

Cockatiels are highly sociable creatures. This means they not only enjoy the company of their owners and fellow cockatiels, they also need company. A lonely cockatiel can act in a destructive manner, get depressed and may even fall physically ill. As long as they haven't been mistreated and have been handled by humans at a young age, cockatiels are sweet, docile and playful.

These birds aren't meant to be placed in a cage merely to be stared at or admired from afar. They love being talked to, played with and touched. Cockatiels will attempt to solicit attention by chirping, climbing on the cage bars, running back and forth, singing, displaying their feathers and exhibiting other attention-grabbing behavior. They may even begin to bang their toys and screech if they don't get the companionship they need.

Show your pet cockatiel affection by rubbing its head, singing or talking to it and taking it out of it cage when it's ready. It's not unusual for these birds to reciprocate your touches by preening your eyebrows, for instance, or giving you gentle pecks with its beak.

Since they're sociable birds even in the wild, cockatiels enjoy eating with the other members of the family, and this includes their human family. Try to include your cockatiel into as many activities at home, as long as it's safe to do so (never leave them alone unattended with young children or other pets like dogs and cats). Have your bird by your side as you surf the Internet, let it perch on your shoulders while you watch your favorite TV show, or enjoy snacking together.

Intelligent Pets

Cockatiels are intelligent birds. While their intelligence is an attractive trait that makes them extra fun and interesting, being smart also means cockatiels need plenty of mental stimulation from their environment and you, their handler. Unhappy birds may exhibit behaviors like nibbling and plucking out their own feathers, even to the point of being stripped bare.

When cockatiels are ignored for too long or too regularly, they are prone to loneliness and depression. And what happens when this bird gets too depressed? It can go as far as refusing to eat and dying from

23

starvation. That's how much company and mental stimulation means to a cockatiel.

As a responsible owner, it's important to keep bird toys in your cockatiel's cage. Pick colorful toys as these attract the bird more than plain looking ones. But do experiment since every bird is unique.

Tip: Be sure to leave a variety of toys but allow your pet to play with only bird-safe toys. Toys meant for other animals, such as cats, may be inappropriate and dangerous for your cockatiel. Often check your pet's toys for signs of wear and tear. Discard any broken toy to keep your cockatiel from harm.

These birds typically enjoy toys they can shred apart or chew on. Other great choices are bird toys they can throw around with their beaks, or pull apart.

Tip: To keep things interesting for your cockatiel, rotate its toys every week. Bring out a group of toys for one week then hide them before taking out a second group of toys for the following week.

Since they're intelligent creatures, cockatiels enjoy exploring. A fun activity for your pet is exploring different rooms inside your home. These birds tend to use their beaks while exploring, especially when examining new objects. Expect a cockatiel to chew often. They'll chew on wood, paper, plastic, cloth, rubber, metal and anything else that catches their fancy. Since chewing is an instinctive behavior for them, you will have to watch over your bird when it's exploring areas outside the cage.

Note: Common items that can prove dangerous for your bird when it chews on them include electric wires, plants, rusty metals, moldy food and anything that contains lead.

Entertaining Companion

As long as you keep a cockatiel happy by providing it plenty of mental stimulation and company, expect these creatures to be entertaining. Even simple acts like watching your pet bird eat, wash itself, preen and play with toys can be very fun for you, the owner.

Many cockatiels can be taught tricks like ringing a bell on command, pulling specific toys and walking up ladders. Being a member of the parrot family, cockatiels may be taught to mimic human words, although keep in mind these birds aren't the fastest learners of speech, especially when compared to other types of parrots like the African Gray. Cockatiels may also learn to sing and mimic non-human sounds, like the ringing of your home telephone. Do expect the sound of a cockatiel to come off as more muffled and unclear than those emitted by larger parrots.

The talking ability of cockatiels is linked to the male hormone testosterone. Because of this correlation between bird-speak and testosterone, male cockatiels are more likely to talk and mimic sounds than their female counterparts. While some females do learn to talk, the chances of a male cockatiel speaking is significantly higher. And what does a talking cockatiel sound like? These birds usually prefer to use a feminine, high-pitched voice.

Expect your pet cockatiel to be quite vocal, especially as soon as they arise in the morning, or when they're about to go to sleep at night. Being sociable creatures, they like saying "good morning" and "good night" to their flock, meaning you and anyone else who lives in the same house.

Cockatiels will be extra noisy if you leave them alone for a while. As soon as you come home, your pet will most likely greet you loudly. It's their way of communicating--it's as if they're letting you know how happy they are to see you return.

Can these birds be demanding? You bet. Like pet dogs or cats, cockatiels can learn to be spoiled and figure out quite quickly how they can get you to do what they want. When this happens and you have a spoiled cockatiel in your hands, excessive screaming can occur—from your bird and perhaps even you!

Don't end up frustrated as a pet owner with a cockatiel who misbehaves. For example, if your cockatiel screams and you come running to their cage to see what it wants, this tells your bird that screaming is effective and will continue to exhibit screeching behavior to get you to come closer each time. The bird will start to think that screaming acts like a "remote control". To keep this from happening, don't give into your bird's demands when it screams or does other unattractive things like banging its toys loudly to get attention.

While it can be a challenge to keep a pet cockatiel from being loud, it's not an impossible feat. Just like owning any intelligent pet, you'll need to exhibit patience and dedicate time. Cockatiels are very much conditioned to love routines and repetitive tasks. Similar to a human baby learning swiftly how crying gets mommy to come to his crib and give him what he wants, a cockatiel will try whatever gets results.

Do introduce your pet cockatiels to healthy routines. If he squawks all the time for attention, don't come running. These birds can be very persistent at times. Some will wear out their owner's patience by simply getting louder and louder until their human gives in. When you're pretty certain your pet is being noisy simply for attention and not because it's ill, get busy doing something else while ignoring the cockatiel.

The whole point is you want to tell your cockatiel that throwing a loud tantrum won't give it what it wants. Perhaps you can go for a walk or relax in front of the TV. This communicates to your pet that you will not surrender to its demands when it acts spoiled and loud.

Tip: Be patient. If your cockatiel is used to you running to do its bidding after a crying spell, it might take several repetitions before your bird adjusts to your new routine of ignoring the crying.

Potential for Fright

Cockatiels experience feelings of fright just like any other pet. The things that alarm these birds the most include loud noises and voices, and also sudden movements. When they're frightened, these birds may react aggressively. They tend to bite, hiss or scream. Some birds may turn away instead, like turn its back towards you or any other source of its fear. It's also not rare to find a scared cockatiel hiding at the bottom part of a cage.

Because we can't avoid certain things that scare these birds such as loud noises, it's advisable to provide your pet places where it can hide in its cage. One way to do this is to have a cage with corners so your cockatiel can hide in one of the corners whenever it feels threatened. Another thing you can do is to tuck the cage in a place far from noise. You can try placing your cockatiel's cage up against a wall, away from hallways, doors, windows and the TV.

As mentioned earlier, cockatiels are prone to experience what's called "night-frights". These frights typically occur when something awakens the bird while it's sleeping at night, causing it to feel extremely startled. A bird going through one of these episodes will typically start to flap its wings rapidly in an effort to fly away from whatever is causing it fear.

There is the potential for danger when night-frights take place because your pet cockatiel can end up with a damaged wing. It can hit anything—be it cage bars, toys and other objects-- while the bird is vigorously flapping its wings out of fright. One way to help avoid night-frights is leaving a soft night light near your pet's cage. Turn this light on each day as soon as it gets dark in the room.

Sources of Stress

Aside from loud noises, there are other sources of stress for cockatiels. These are moody birds that generally dislike change. They love routine, probably because routine spells out security.

Even minor changes like changing the color of the curtains in the room where your cockatiel lives can stress it out. Many pet owners notice their cockatiels get stressed when the owner wears new cologne. Some cockatiels dislike strangers so much they will screech when an unfamiliar person visits. The birds may act aggressively even after the visitor leaves. These pets also don't like it when you change routines at home.

When cockatiels are stressed, their immune system gets compromised, increasing the risk of getting physically ill through infections and other diseases. Furthermore, unhealthy, malnourished and stressed out pet birds can get sick if their cage is located in a drafty area. Spots with moving air tend to provide these birds an environment with constantly changing temperature, plus varying temperatures in different areas of the cage.

Most birds are unable to withstand a temperature drop of 10 or more degrees Fahrenheit within a 24-hour period. A cockatiel experiencing rapid temperature drops can get very sick. Keeping your pet bird well nourished and stress-free makes them less prone to getting ill from drafts. But even a mostly healthy bird may experience stress without you being aware so it's always best to keep bird cages away from drafty spots in your home.

Tip: How do you know if a spot has draft? Hold a candle and light it up in the area. If you see the flame flickering then chances are good it's a drafty spot, definitely not a good choice for your cockatiel's cage location.

Females Versus Males

Should you get a male or female pet? Is there a difference between the personalities of a typical male cockatiel and that of a female? Generally, yes, although there are exceptions. Remember, no two birds are completely alike in temperament, and this is especially true for an intelligent and sociable creature like the cockatiel.

Females tend to act more nervous than their male counterparts, but they also have a higher chance of being friendlier and more affectionate than males. It's more difficult to teach a female how to talk but they do chirp in a charmingly friendly and sing-song way.

Male cockatiels have bigger bodies than females and, like the majority of bird species, often have brighter and more colorful feathers than the girls. The males can act more aggressive than females and the likelihood of being bitten is higher with a male cockatiel over a female one. There is also more exhibition of typical hormonal aggressive behavior from the boys, even when no female is in sight.

The good news about male cockatiels is they do sing and talk more. They're surprisingly better at parenting than the females. While the mommy cockatiels are in charge of hatching the eggs and caring for their newborns, the males don't leave and abandon the babies. When experiencing fatherhood, male cockatiels become very protective of their young, especially in the wild where predators abound. The males can be considered nurturing and warm towards their offspring. In situations where the mother cockatiel is injured or killed, the father typically steps in and fulfills its role as a parent capably and willingly.

An important thing you must know if you choose a female cockatiel is that, even without a mate, they are prone to laying unfertilized eggs. These eggs don't house a baby cockatiel and will never hatch. This can pose a risk to your pet's health.

If she ends up egg-bound, your cockatiel may need emergency medical attention from an avian vet. If she lays egg chronically, you will need to bring her to a vet as well.

Dusty Animals

Cockatiels produce plenty of dust, otherwise known as powder down. The birds produce the down naturally. Compared to many other bird species, a cockatiel's body has plenty of down, making them one of the dustiest pet birds to own.

Expect to find white powder all over your pet's living quarters-- this includes their cage and any object situated near the cage. When a cockatiel shakes out its feathers, you'll see a cloud of the dusty down. Don't be surprised to see a coating of white powder on your skin after you've pet your cockatiel. If you have allergies or asthma, find out beforehand if a cockatiel is something you can own. Handle someone's pet cockatiel before making a commitment to owning one.

Even though misty baths can get rid of some of the bird's down, it's practically impossible to get rid of all of the powder.

Anyone allergic to the down is better off with a different type of pet. If asthma or allergies are present in you or someone in your household, it's best to speak with a doctor before bringing any bird home.

Costs of Owning a Cockatiel

The cost of owning a small bird as a pet can quickly add up. The total price tag can be more than what you initially expected. Don't acquire a pet cockatiel under the false assumption that it will cost less than a cat or a dog. Don't assume it will take up less of your time than other pets.

A cockatiel will need a bigger cage than a canary or other smaller pet birds. It will also require more handling and bonding time than plenty of other pets like a fish or a turtle. These birds will need a steady supply of food, durable toys and some basic training.

Some of the beginner items you'll need for a pet cockatiel are listed below (For more details, read the chapter **Supplies and Accessories):**

- Bird cage

- Bag of bird food

- Several toys

- Food and water bowls

- Swing

- Ladder

- Perches

- Bird bath

- Nail clipper

- Travel carrier

- Cleaning supplies

The cost you're expected to spend as a beginner cockatiel owner ranges anywhere from $300 to $1,000.

Even a relatively inexpensive bird like a cockatiel will need a financial commitment from you, the owner. Keep in mind, too, the additional expenses you will incur during your bird's life. These will include tests at the vet's office, such as tests for psittacosis, and vaccinations and perhaps micro-chipping. Other expenses you must expect to pay for throughout owning a pet cockatiel are bird seeds and pellets, treats, fruits and vegetables, vitamin supplements, cage and bird cleaning supplies, toys and routine exams at the vet. Your cockatiel will typically need vaccinations and wing-clippings.

Before deciding to bring a cockatiel back into your home for yourself and the rest of your family, make a careful decision to figure out if you can afford one—both financially and time-wise. Don't make an impulse buy, only to be unable to provide the kind of environment that will keep you and the bird happy and healthy. All types of pets need a certain degree of time and money.

Dispelling Myths

Here are some common myths about pet cockatiels. Knowing more about these wonderful creatures will help you determine whether it's the right pet for your or not. Remember, these birds can live for over 15 and even 20 years. The decision to get one is a big one that you shouldn't take lightly.

Myth #1: Cockatiels won't require a lot of my time.

Cockatiels are time-consuming pets. They require plenty of time bonding with their owner. This includes time outside its cage playing, talking, and staying by your side while enjoying your company. Neglected birds get very stressed and may fall ill and experience depression.

Myth #2: Its cage won't require plenty of cleaning.

Cockatiels love to drop seeds, pellets and other food on the floor. These birds enjoy shaking their heads and playing with food. If that means food gets thrown around, so be it. They also produce a lot of powder down. You will have to clean your cockatiel's cage daily if you want to keep yourself and your bird healthy. Ensure its living quarters are as bacteria-free as possible.

Myth #3: All cockatiels are friendly and gentle.

While most handfed cockatiels that have been handled by humans at a young age are very sweet and even tempered, an unhappy or untamed bird can behave in an aloof and even aggressive manner. Yes, they love bonding with their owners but you have to dedicate time and patience before earning your cockatiel's trust. With dedication and a cockatiel that has been human-handled early, it can be one of the most loving and sweet pet birds to own.

A Cockatiel and the Rest of the Family

It's smarter to acquire a pet cockatiel for an entire family, as opposed to buying one for a child. Families with children aged 5 years or less are better off waiting until the children are a little bit older before bringing home a cockatiel. These birds can be very moody and will react negatively towards loud noises and sudden movements, elements that younger children are sure to provide. Chances are, the energetic movements and voices of toddlers will provide stress rather than a positive experience for most cockatiels.

Compared to many other parrots, cockatiels have small beaks but they can still deliver a mean bite. Their bites can break skin and cause bleeding. It's not rare for a cockatiel to clamp down with their beaks, refusing to release the bite quickly. When it feels threatened, a cockatiel's bite can stay on like a hard grip for several seconds.

Cockatiels can make wonderful pets for older children who understand and know how to handle the animal gently and respectfully. These birds can be tamed with ease. They enjoy spending time with humans outside of the cage habitat. They don't just tolerate human attention--they crave and enjoy our company immensely.

These birds have the tendency to become one-person pets if they don't get used to being handled by other members of the family. The more people at home play with the cockatiel, the better. Thanks to social activities from different people, your bird will less likely bite or act aggressively out of fear.

If you have responsible older children, the daily care a cockatiel needs can be accomplished by the whole family. The children can take care of washing the bird's bowls, cleaning the cage and providing bird feeds. No matter what age your children are, always provide parental supervision and monitor your children as they fulfill their pet owner duties. Accomplishing these chores together will bring you closer as a family and help everyone bond with your charming pet.

Chapter 2: Supplies and Accessories

In the first chapter, we discussed how cockatiels can be one of the most affectionate and entertaining pets around. Small, very intelligent and sociable, a happy bird will bring hours of entertainment and companionship to the right owner and household.

The bird's warm and engaging personality makes it very trainable. It's no wonder cockatiels are some of the most popular pet birds. When cared for properly by the right handler, these birds are fascinating and unforgettable.

Inexperienced bird owners who are willing to invest time learning about these birds can own a pet cockatiel. The vital thing is that you're aware of its needs, including its keen need to socialize. Since cockatiels have natural playful and friendly personalities, they will only thrive with an owner who's able to spend time with them.

Other than a cockatiel's desire to bond with other family members, just like any pet, it has specific needs in terms of food, housing, bedding, health and fun. This chapter will cover the supplies you the pet owner will have to provide your bird.

From details on the right cage size for your feathery friend to the type of food it requires to lead a healthy and long life, in this section you'll learn what to prepare at home before welcoming a cockatiel. The goal is to be prepared as early as possible so you and your cockatiel will get to spend several happy years together.

Cage Requirements

The first thing you're going to need before you bring home your pet cockatiel is a cage that has enough room for your new housemate. Generally speaking, these birds are most comfortable in the type of cage they're used to. If you're acquiring your bird from a previous owner directly, ask for the cage the cockatiel's already lived in. This will lessen the stress from the move.

Tip: If the previous cage is too small, you should upgrade it to one with a more suitable size (which we will discuss in a moment) but during your bird's first few days adjusting to your home, it helps to house it in the enclosure the bird's used to. Young cockatiels are good at adapting. Eventually they'll grow to like any cage after an adjustment period.

Fortunately, when it comes to enclosures, there are a few options that are suitable for these birds. You can choose to place your cockatiel outside or inside your house. Pre-made versions of either kind of dwellings may be purchased. The ideal temperature is 70 to 80 degrees fahrenheit. They can tolerate higher & lower, but those are comfortable ranges medians. If you live in a considerably warmer or colder area, you may want to keep them indoors or possibly indoors depending on the season.

Another option is building your new pet's living quarters in a room indoors, or from an alcove. Big store-bought powder-coated cages meant for parrots are also excellent choices. Cages you can find for sale can range from very simple wire cages to fancy looking varieties. When it comes to narrowing down your choices, think about some factors to help you find the best match.

Price

When it comes to cockatiel cages and other enclosures, the price range falls between an average of $50 (for the minimum size suitable for cockatiels) to over $100 for a large cage suitable to house one or two birds. An aviary will cost around $300.

Comfort

Expect your new pet to explore and perch at the top portion of any type of cage you provide. Because of this natural cockatiel tendency, it's best to go with long cages rather than tall ones. In the eyes of these birds, it's the length of the cage that matters. The longer the cage, the roomier it will feel for a cockatiel.

It's typical for cockatiels to spend most of its hours enclosed at the top portion of the cage. Don't choose a cage shorter than two feet in length. Your bird will be happier and healthier when it has sufficient room for fun and exercise.

Bar Spacing

Cockatiels are very inquisitive little creatures. They love to explore and tinker with objects. This means choosing the wrong kind of cage can be dangerous for your bird. Cockatiels are prone to be curious about the other side of the cage bars. They seem to always be itching to go out and play with something located just outside their enclosure. Because of this, choose a cage with bar spacing that is close together—one that's close enough so your pet won't be able to get its head through the bars.

Tip: As a rule, cage with bars that are half an inch to three-quarters of an inch apart are ideal choices.

Always check for the material of the cage bars. Look to see if they're made of safe materials. A simple aviary wire does the job of housing a bird well but if your cockatiel were to chew on the wire, it could get zinc poisoning. To prevent this from happening, always wash new cages or wires using a vinegar solution before housing any bird inside.

It's vital to check the materials of any enclosure you prepare for your cockatiel since poisoning is always a possibility. Zinc poisoning is a type of heavy-metal poisoning. Vets can give emergency medical attention to birds experiencing zinc or lead poisoning. Instead of relying on emergency care, however, it's best to remember the adage "an ounce of prevention is better than a pound of cure". Make an effort not to expose your pet to risky cage materials.

Be on the lookout for cast-iron cages. Some of these are welded with lead solder, a dangerous material for your bird. Cockatiels love to chew or nibble on just about anything around them and chewing on cast-iron wires may lead to heavy metal poisoning.

Tip: How will you know if a cage is lead-free? Use a lead test kit, one typically used to check items for child-safety.

The majority of big cast iron cages are made with a durable industrial finish known as powder coating. There have been reports of this type of cage containing zinc. When your pet ends up chewing off the coating of these enclosures, poisoning can follow.

Unfortunately, unlike lead tests, home tests for zinc aren't something you can buy. To find out about zinc-content on a particular cage you're interested in, get in touch with the cage's manufacturer and inquire about the paint used on the item. If you already own a cage and are worried it contains zinc, you have the option of sending samples to a lab for safety testing.

Cleaning

If you want to make your life easier as a pet bird owner in the long haul, consider the amount of cleaning a potential enclosure will require. Cages shaped like rectangles are generally easier to clean than round ones. Round cages make folding newspapers to line the bottom extra difficult.

If possible, select a cage that comes with a grate. The grate keeps the bird away from fallen food and droppings. Having a deep tray located beneath the grate makes daily cleaning tasks far less arduous.

You might have noticed cages that come with shields that extend out from the cage. The good thing about these shields is how they keep your cockatiel's droppings away from the floor. On the flipside, the droppings end up on the shield that will need to be cleaned often.

Choose a cage with a big door so reaching into the cage for whatever reason is as easy as possible. The best cages allow you to reach every nook inside through the door. If you're going for some of the bigger cages, keep in mind that the only way to completely clean the larger ones is with a hose.

More about Cage Door

We can't stress enough how it'll make your life much easier if you go with a cockatiel cage that has a large front door. Compared to other small birds, cockatiels are quite large. A cage with a small door meant for a parakeet isn't a good choice for a cockatiel.

Whenever anyone needs to reach inside the cage, especially during the daily cleaning required, you will see how a roomy cage definitely makes the task easier. It's wonderful to have enough space to maneuver your hand around the cage, thanks to a big cage door. You'll also find cages that come with doors that convert to perches, making it unnecessary to purchase additional cage-top perch equipment.

Having extra openings in an enclosure can also help. This is especially true if you plan on breeding cockatiels in the future. Choosing a cage equipped with an opening located high in the cage is excellent because you can attach a nesting box there. Without a pre-built opening, you'll have to cut a hole in the cage in order to attach the nesting box, giving you extra work and the possibility of a ruined cage.

Food and Water in the Cage

Keep your cockatiel's water and food bowls in a spot inside the cage that is easily accessible from outside. It's a great idea to have a minimum of three bowls for your bird: one for water, the second bowl for feeds and a third bowl for vegetables.

Tip: You can add a fourth bowl for treats if you wish. You'll find the majority of parrot cages are sold with only two bowls. Purchase an additional one, plus treat cups.

Safety in Mind

Always make safety your number one priority when choosing your cockatiel's cage. No matter how pretty some ornaments look, if they aren't made to be safe toys for cockatiels, it's best to skip them as they can be dangerous for your bird.

These energetic and playful pets can wedge a wing in tight places. Steer clear of round cages designed with wire bars, especially when the bars narrow in some places. This type of enclosure is extra dangerous for birds as the creature can get a foot or a wing stuck in any narrow opening.

When making the final decision regarding your cockatiel's enclosure, look at the housing from the eyes of a curious bird. Imagine the potential trouble your pet can get into while inside its living quarters. Go for the enclosure the poses the least number of risks.

Cage Location

Think of the cage as your bird's universe. This is the spot where the cockatiel will spend the majority of its time. The cage protects and shields your pet, as well as protects your own things from the inquisitive nature of the cockatiel. With its curious tendencies to explore, plus is sharp beak, these birds can destroy furniture or décor in a quick minute.

When choosing where to place your cockatiel's cage, pick a spot where the bird can be close to where plenty of family activities occur. Don't put the cage right in the middle of any hustle and bustle, however. While cockatiels are very sociable, loud noises and sudden movements stress them out.

Cockatiels are known to get very comfortable living in cages placed against a wall. This way it can watch activities going on inside the room and not feel insecure, worried that someone might sneak up behind the cage.

Another factor to consider is the amount of irregular activities occurring in a location. Don't place your cockatiel's cage in places where they may easily feel surprised. This includes areas with blind spots. A person suddenly coming into view can startle your bird.

When it comes to windows, don't place your bird's cage near a spot that gets too much natural heat from the sun. You don't want the sun overheating your pet. It's a good idea to place the cage close to a window if you want to keep your bird entertained. Birds will enjoy watching the activity taking place outside.

The kitchen is a terrible choice for any bird cage. There is a huge risk your cockatiel will breathe in poisonous fumes. The smoke emitted from nonstick cookware, for instance, can act like a high dose of air pollution to any bird. Place the cage in a spot where you and the rest of the members of your household like to hang out.

Keep the bottom part of the cage lined with newspaper or some other safe product. After doing so to a clean cage, the cage is now ready to be called home.

Housing Supplies

After you have found a suitable cage for your cockatiel, the next step is to provide other supplies. Your new friend is going to need more than a roof over its head in order to thrive.

Here are the basic housing supplies to keep your cockatiel happy, healthy and as stress-free as possible.

Bowls

Your cockatiel will require a minimum of three bowls. One bowl is for the water, another for dry food like seeds, and the third bowl is for moist or wet food. You might also want to add a fourth bowl to keep treats in.

When choosing the bowls, the safest option is to use bowls specifically for parrots. Cockatiels love to chew and a cheap plastic bowl that's not meant for birds may introduce a toxic source of chemicals to your pet.

Toys

Cockatiels certainly enjoy chewing. Giving your bird access to bird-friendly toys will keep them happy. Chewing and being curious are natural tendencies in these creatures and proving them an outlet for these inclinations will help keep their stress levels down. Bored cockatiels tend to act out. They may pick their own feathers when highly stressed.

Only purchase toys that are marked safe for cockatiels. Your pet may quickly choke from playing with an inappropriate toy. Bird toys made with palm strips, twig balls and natural vegetable-tanned leather materials are excellent choices. Cockatiels, like larger birds, also enjoy wooden toys. Do make sure not to choose one that is made for a much larger bird species. Your cockatiel might not be able to chew on a toy that's too big. Cheap and safe toy options include brand new popsicle sticks and balsa wood. Balled up paper works as a homemade toy, too.

To make sure your pet is far from feeling boredom—which can lead to depression—provide it plenty of chances to forage. In the wild, cockatiels take foraging very seriously. In captivity, the opportunity to forage provides these birds with mental stimulation and physical activity.

Check your pet's toys and accessories often, as frequently as every day. Any worn or damaged toy should be thrown away as these can cause injury to your cockatiel. It's a great habit to rotate your bird's toys as it's normal for these creatures to find their toys boring after a period.

When your pet isn't paying a toy any more attention, hide it for a few days and place different toys to take the previous toy's place. Avoid putting an unfamiliar toy inside a cockatiel's dwelling place without doing an initial introduction. Try to introduce new items in a neutral location so your bird won't feel stressed out in its own cage, thanks to a new and strange item in its eyes. If you have a new toy for your cockatiel, place it for a few days just outside the bird cage. Give your pet enough time to get used to the new toys and accessories.

Many cockatiel owners think mirrors are good toys for their birds. On the contrary, mirrors don't make appropriate toys because these creatures are prone to bond with their own reflections. Birds see their own image as another bird. This is especially true for cockatiels kept alone. You, the owner, will have a more challenging time bonding with and training your pet if a mirror is provided. Two or more cockatiels kept in the same cage won't need a mirror at all because they have each other for company and games.

Perches

The type of perches you provide your cockatiel will matter a lot. Imagine being on your feet all hours of the day, just like this bird. Wouldn't you want to stand on the most comfortable surface possible? The kind of perches in the cage plays a huge role in the comfort and health of your pet. Cockatiels require different types of sizes and textures when it comes to their perches. The right perches will give your pet the proper kind of exercise for its feet. For an animal that spends all of its years on its toes, so to speak, the health of their legs are of utmost importance.

You'll find plenty of bird perches available in the market. They come in varieties like durable plastic, wood, rope and concrete. Some perches even resemble ladders to make things extra interesting for the birds. Some perches are designed to go straight across, while others are built to go diagonally. The different directions provide various ways for the cockatiel to climb, keeping it active and entertained.

Give your pet access to natural branches. A terrific example is a Manzanita perch since this will give your pet different widths to rest on. The varying width makes it easy for your pet to exercise its feet. In the wild, most branches aren't built in perfectly straight lines. Try to emulate the natural perches by providing branches as perches.

Before you grab any branch outdoors to use as a perch for your cockatiel, keep in mind some random branch pulled out of your neighborhood may contain all kinds of pesticides that are used to treat trees. Make sure your source for a natural branch is a pesticide-free tree. Clean any branch thoroughly. Never add a natural branch without washing it prior to putting it inside your cockatiel's home.

To clean natural tree branches, cut each branch to a size suitable for your pet's cage. Scrub to clean the branch, washing it in a solution made of 10 parts water and one-part bleach. Rinse the new perch thoroughly with water. Next, set your oven to 200 degrees Fahrenheit and heat any branch for 45 minutes.

You may also use a perch to dull your cockatiel's nails, saving you some grooming time. Look for a bird-grooming perch. These are typically made of concrete. You'll also find a variety that has a sand-blasted finish. Don't provide any more than one bird-grooming perch per cage. You don't want your cockatiel's feet to always be perched on an abrasive material.

The only way to find out if your bird will like a particular perch is by testing the perch out with the cockatiel. In terms of size, a good size for a perch is one where the toes of your bird wrap ½ to ¾ inches of the way around its perch. It should have a diameter of one to one and a half inches.

Tip: If your find your pet's toes touch around the perch, this means the perch's diameter is too small. If, however, the bird's toes lie flat on its perch, this means the perch is way too wide.

Lighting

As many new cockatiel owners experience, the middle of the night can bring in some frightening sounds. If you're unaware or new to the common cockatiel phenomenon known as "night-frights" then you just might be as frightened as your pet. Night-frights are very common among these birds. The cockatiel may start to thrash around and often screech loudly when these episodes occur.

In most cases, something in the dark alarmed the bird and caused it to experience night-fright. The trigger can be a shadow or a noise. In an effort to protect itself, a cockatiel will attempt to take off in flight, only to end up thrashing around its cage out of panic. Plenty of cockatiels sustain injuries due to thrashing about from night-frights.

To reduce night-frights, place a night light close to your cockatiel's cage. See how your bird reacts to the light and allow it several nights to get used to the change. Since each bird is different, your pet may require a longer duration to feel less stressed at night. If you find your cockatiel hasn't adjusted to the night light after a week and the night-frights haven't disappeared, perhaps your pet might prefer its cage to be covered in complete darkness. See what works and adjust the lighting situation for your cockatiel according to its personal reaction.

If the lighting adjustments don't reduce the cockatiel's night-frights, you will have to do some evaluation and figure out your pet's personal preferences. See if you can find and then eliminate the source of the frights. It can be a cat stalking your pet, bright headlights that flash a window at night, or it might be a certain sound that occurs only in the evening.

Tip: If your pet continues to thrash at night, you might want to consider setting up another cage just for night-time use--one without toys or perches to lessen the injury the cockatiel might sustain from acting in panic. Line the cage with towels for extra cushion and protection.

And as for the type of light to have during your cockatiel's waking hours, a full-spectrum light situated above its cage is a great source of Vitamin D. Incandescent full-spectrum bulbs are good choices and work well if you have free space for a lamp right next to your pet's cage. Many types of windows unfortunately filter out natural Vitamin D from the sun, making additional lights necessary. When installing lighting fixtures, keep cords out of your bird's reach. Remember birds require approximately 10 to 12 hours of rest daily.

Food and Nutrition

The most crucial thing to remember when you're planning a cockatiel's diet is variety. When it comes to food, these wonderful creatures are smart and sociable enough to let you know what it likes, what it hates and what it simply can't get enough of.

Don't ever force a cockatiel to eat food it doesn't enjoy. Leave it to your pet to choose what it will eat. If your bird eats just a tiny portion of any other type of food besides its usual seeds and pellet, that's normal as well. The important thing, after all, is the presence of variety in your pet's diet.

Eating Habits

When these birds consume table foods, they end up eating fewer pellets. Birds are prone to eating as much food as their bodies need and nothing more. Cockatiels eat about 15 grams of high energy food each day. Your goal as the pet owner is to feed your bird 15 grams of nutrient-rich food daily.

Aside from pellets, give your cockatiel a wide array of healthy foods each day so it gets to eat a balanced and healthy diet. Learn about the toxic foods you should never serve your cockatiel. These can make your pet sick and even lead to death.

Toxic Foods

The following are the most commonly found toxic foods for cockatiels (*Bear in mind this isn't a complete list. There may be other common household items not listed here that can harm your pet, if in doubt don't feed it and talk with a vet*):

- Rhubarb
- Avocados
- Potato leaves and stems
- Tomato
- Alcohol
- Eggplant
- Coffee
- Tea
- Bean plants

- Chocolate

- Salt

- Sugar

- Oily foods

- Fruit seeds or pits (especially those from apricots, apples, oranges, peaches, cherries, plums and pears)

- Tobacco

Don't feed cockatiels shellfish like crabs, shrimps or lobsters. These contain high amounts of bacterial contamination. Common bacteria found in shellfish are generally safe for us to eat but may prove toxic to birds.

Fruits and Vegetables

When giving your pet veggies and fruits, make the portions small and, whenever possible, serve the produce shredded, chopped or cut into tiny pieces. The small size will motivate most cockatiels to grab and try a wide array of fruits and vegetables.

When serving produce, thoroughly wash every veggie and fruit before offering any to your pet. You want to make sure none of its food contains pesticides and other harmful chemicals.

Tip: To clean fruits and vegetables properly, soak them in a bowl of cold water. Allow the produce to soak for a few minutes. Afterwards, rinse off with fresh water before giving them to your cockatiel.

Certain vegetables are not toxic to cockatiels but they provide very low amounts of vitamins and minerals. Examples of such nutritionally poor veggies are celery, iceberg lettuce and cucumbers. These are mainly comprised of water and don't contain much nutrients. If your pet happens to love these water-rich varieties, provide them as occasional treats.

When choosing the most nutrient-dense vegetables, go for those with vibrant orange hues, as well as dark green vegetables. These contain the most amounts of vitamins.

Certain vegetables are best served moderately, once or twice each week and no more. Varieties like spinach and parsley have oxalic acid, a type of acid that binds with calcium. Consuming these veggies can lead to less calcium being absorbed in the bird's body, stressing out the kidneys. Serving your pet a diet rich in oxalic acid may lead to poor blood clotting and even convulsions. Even low amounts of oxalates can cause decreased growth, poor bone health and painful kidney stones.

While you don't have to completely eliminate all produce containing oxalic acid from your cockatiel's diet, remember to serve them no more than two times in a week. Other veggies containing oxalic acid—although in smaller amounts—are carrots, beet greens, collard greens, turnips, berries and lettuce.

Veggies like broccoli have phytate or phytic acid. These phytates can cause the same side effects as oxalic acid does, leading to decreased calcium absorption in the cockatiel. The absorption of essential zinc and iron are known to also get decreased in the process, depriving your bird of these necessary nutrients.

Many green vegetables are comprised with large amounts of water, some made of 90 percent water. Serving too much green vegetables per day can lead to excess urine in the cockatiel.

Traces of phytates can be found in legumes, broccoli, carrots, nuts, potatoes, carrots, green beans, berries and sweet potatoes. Always serve these in moderation, no more than two times in a week.

Plenty of sugar can be found in carrots and sweet potatoes. A diet rich in sugar can lead to yeast infections in the bird. You can serve these foods as occasional treats. If you decide to give your cockatiel grapes or strawberries, remember these fruits rot swiftly. Discard any discolored, bruised or mushy produce right away, keeping your bird's home clean and free of fungal and bacterial infections.

When attempting to serve a cockatiel a balanced diet with variety, keep in mind which foods should only be served once or twice weekly. Every day, provide a fresh supply of fruits and vegetables to your bird. Try not to serve the same type of food each day.

Because plenty of fruits and veggies that cockatiels love are sources of an enzyme inhibitor or a natural toxin such as those mentioned above, it's crucial to aim for variety in the pet's diet. Serving a wide array of food ensures your cockatiel gets all kinds of nutrients. A selection of fresh foods daily will provide your bird the best nutritional sources.

Great choices for vegetables are:

- Spinach
- Sprouts
- Turnip Greens
- Mustard Greens
- Swiss chard

- Chicory

- Broccoli

- Escarole

- Tomatoes

- Bok Choy

- Beet Greens

- Collard greens

- Grated Carrots

- Corn on the Cob

- Kale

- Endive

- Yams

- Sweet potato

- Pumpkin

Cockatiels love the following fruits:

- Mangos

- Apples

- Nectarines

- Apricots

- Papayas

- Bananas

- Peaches

- Grapes

- Oranges

- Cantaloupe

Note: Never give your cockatiel fruits with seeds because some seeds can be highly toxic. One example is the pits of cherries. These have trace amounts of cyanide.

Pellets or Seeds?

While many people like to argue and pick sides--choosing between either pellets or seeds as the best food for cockatiels--a good reminder regarding balance and variety in your cockatiel's diet is key. Provided your pet is getting a variety of foods, there is no need to feed it just either pellets or seeds. You can feed both to your bird.

If you feed your cockatiel seeds, always keep the seed tray clean. Wash the tray with soapy hot water to keep it from growing fungus and bacteria. Before serving seeds, make sure the seed tray is totally dry. The presence of moisture on a seed tray provides a healthy breeding ground for harmful fungus and bacteria, something you and your bird won't be very happy about.

Cockatiels like to get seed from the husks. Because of this feeding habit, you are likely to find the bird's bowl filled with empty husks that your pet didn't eat. Be on the lookout for rotting or discarded food and keep the seed tray clean and filled with fresh seeds.

When purchasing a bag of seeds at any pet store, place the seeds in your freezer when you get home to keep them fresh and bug-free. Keep the seeds in a sealed or re-sealable bag so moisture doesn't enter. By keeping your seeds in the freezer, they will remain fresh for several months.

Water

A cockatiel's water source must be always kept clean. Change the water bowl every day, plus any time the water becomes dirty. Food and bird droppings may fall into the water bowl. Keep water trays washed and cleaned using soapy hot water. This helps keep bacteria and fungus from growing and infection your bird.

Protein

Is it fine to feed cockatiels meat? Yes, as long as your pet only eats tiny amounts. Cockatiels can eat very limited servings of beef, chicken or fish. Another excellent source of protein for your bird is cooked chicken eggs. You can serve them scrambled or hard boiled. See if your bird enjoys yogurt or cottage cheese—other wonderful sources of protein.

When serving your cockatiel meat or eggs, it's advisable to serve only freshly cooked meat and eggs. Avoid giving your pet fish, eggs or meat that have already been refrigerated then re-heated. As for raw dried beans, oats, rice, barley, sweet potatoes, beets and turnips, these have enzyme-inhibitors that may disrupt a cockatiel's digestive system temporarily. Cook these before serving, in order to deactivate harmful compounds.

Chapter 3: Taming and Training

The personality of each individual cockatiel, especially how it relates and reacts to people, depends plenty on the animal's previous experience. Cockatiels that weren't socialized early on, or those that weren't hand-fed and hand-tamed, as well as birds who have experienced abuse or neglect, will be very mistrustful around people. It's not that rare for birds with adverse past experiences to bite. Taming a pet that bites is definitely a frustrating path for anyone, even for experienced cockatiel owners.

There are cockatiels that are quick to respond to human handlers in an affectionate and gentle way, enjoying the company of people. Other birds may take weeks, months and even years before they warm up to people.

Bringing a New Cockatiel Home

Any cockatiel will experience an adjustment phase when it moves to a new home. Even the most confident and hand-tamed bird will feel some levels of stress since birds don't like change. If your new cockatiel seems frightened of you at first and is acting stressed out in its new environment, remember this is normal behavior. Most birds take several days, or even weeks, to adapt to a new home.

If the cockatiel you bring home hasn't been used to hand-feeding or taming, there's a good chance the bird will hiss or turn away when you approach its cage. It may even try to bite you if you place a hand nearby.

For older birds that have been neglected, they will act more territorial and possibly aggressive. Any cockatiel that acts frightened should never be taken out of its cage during the first week. Give it time to adjust after the move.

If you brought home a young cockatiel, especially one that has been recently weaned and is used to being handfed and tamed, then you should bring the bird out of the cage the same day you introduce it to your home. This is to keep a well-socialized cockatiel from becoming fearful or cage-bound.

Even if you have brought home a friendly new cockatiel for a pet, it's best not to have visitors around during the first week. Allow your bird to initially bond with you and members of your household first.

When bonding with a new cockatiel:

1. Sit next to its cage while the bird is safely inside. Spend time talking to it softly for approximately 15 minutes.

2. Do other activities away from the bird afterwards, allowing it to observe you from afar and furthermore letting it get used to its new home.

3. Repeat this routine several times each day during the first week.

4. After the first week is up, avoid putting your hand inside the cage just yet. Be patient. Neither should you grab the cockatiel with a towel, pushing it to leave its cage before the bird is ready and relaxed. By acting hasty this way, the bird may bite and lose any trust you earned during the initial week.

5. Let the cockatiel come to you on its own terms. Wait for the bird to approach you. The time this will take all depends on your particular pet's personality. With patience, time and gentleness, your new cockatiel will soon approach your hand, ready to get a taste of whatever yummy food you're holding.

6. Spend as much time sitting next to your bird's cage as possible. The more fearful it's acting, the more time you should invest earning the cockatiel's trust. Read a

book next to the cage, or surf the Internet while sitting with your computer or tablet beside the bird's dwelling place. Eat your food while sitting next to your cockatiel's personal nook.

7. Speak to your cockatiel every day. Use a soft, slow and affectionate tone. Since these birds are sociable, flocking creatures, they do require plenty of interaction from you. Be consistent in talking to your cockatiel and, before you know it, your pet will start to become interested in your voice.

8. Offer treats and other food while speaking to your bird. Don't stick your hand inside the cage. If your cockatiel isn't acting aggressive around you when you sit and talk to it, take a piece of food you know it enjoys and place it between your fingers. Offer the food through the cage bars. Providing treats while speaking to the bird will help it associate your voice with the positive and enjoyable experience of eating.

9. Once your cockatiel is comfortable enough to accept treats from your hand, make sure its wings are clipped (Read Chapter 4 to know more about this grooming task) so you can leave its cage door open. Give him snacks like seeds from your open palm, always letting

the cockatiel come to you when it's ready. Just like dogs, food motivates cockatiels and offering your bird food by hand is a very powerful way to earn its trust.

A Cockatiel's Bite

Like almost all pets, young cockatiels are the easier to work than adults when you're trying to tame your bird. As soon as you begin training, it's critical to keep in mind why a pet might bite. When it comes to birds, biting is their response to what they perceive to be a threat. In the cockatiel's eyes, the biting is always brought about by a provoking factor. The bird assumes there is no other way to defend itself or escape the perceived danger.

Learn how to handle and tame your cockatiel by knowing as much as you can about biting. This is one of the first things you must tackle when it comes to interacting with your pet. This is not due to cockatiels being known for biting—when handled regularly and properly, cockatiels are some of the most affectionate birds around—but so that you the owner can begin on a positive note with your pet as early as possible.

To an inexperienced or new pet owner, not being knowledgeable about the pet's biting tendencies can easily trigger frustrations, lack of affection towards the animal and may enforce negative patterns that will last throughout the relationship with the animal. The more you know about biting and how to deal with this unwanted behavior, the more you and your cockatiel will experience a positive dynamic together.

What Causes the Biting

Your cockatiel doesn't have massive claws, fangs, teeth or a bulky mass so it resorts to biting as the swiftest way it can defend its body or territory. When it comes to birds, threats make their instinctive nature react. They often prefer to leave a dangerous scene and would rather not fight the threat in return.

Fighting other birds and delivering bites are not natural tendencies of cockatiels in the wild. Out in nature, all parrots use their beaks in order to climb, eat, create nests and feed their young. It is common for these birds in the wild, however, to instinctively display aggressive behavior like biting when they're attempting to defend their home and safety. Cockatiels kept as pets exhibit the same defensive tactics.

Survival or fear biting happens when a cockatiel senses a threat and feels it needs to defend itself or its dwelling area. Fear is the most common reason leading to these birds biting. Cockatiels tend to frighten pretty easily. They don't like change as this spells out lack of security for them. You can quickly destroy your relationship with your bird if you attempt to frighten it, even in jest. What is a sign of affection and a fun activity for you is a life-threatening situation for the cockatiel.

Don't just stick your hand inside your bird's cage in an effort to grab it. In most cases, cockatiel pet owners get bitten because of the bird's fear of hands and fingers, especially if you move suddenly or haven't spent enough time earning the cockatiel's trust.

Fear may also be caused by objects above the cockatiel's cage, like light fixtures, hanging decorations and ceiling fans. These birds don't appreciate sudden or jerky movements, and the most common sources of such movements are children, dogs and other animals. A hamster looking cute while running on a wheel may not be appreciated by a cockatiel. Don't let a pet cat stare at your cockatiel's cage, even if the kitty is simply looking. The presence of any cat is enough to scare most birds.

It's normal for pet birds to act fearfully and possibly bite in the presence of big crowds, strangers and anyone who approaches the cockatiel from behind. Plenty of these birds are fearful of gruff voices, yelling, high-pitched tones of very young children, dogs barking, doors slamming, wild animal sounds, fireworks and other loud or threatening sounds.

Fear may also be provoked within cockatiels because of changes occurring in their environment. A move to a new cage or placing its old cage in a new location can trigger fear and stress, which in turn can possibly lead to fear biting.

Even objects meant for your pet's enjoyment--like new toys, fresh perches or strange foods--can threaten its feelings of security. Changes in the room where you keep the cockatiel's cage can also lead to fearful feelings in your pet. If you've installed new curtains or furniture, or if you're wearing a new shirt or perfume, and your bird is acting fearful and nippy, chances are the change is stressing it out.

Give your bird enough time to adapt to changes. If you place your cockatiel in a new cage or location, for instance, give the bird time alone to relax. Approach your little friend by speaking to it in a friendly tone and offering treats. Never stick your hand suddenly inside its cage, especially when changes have recently been introduced to your pet's environment.

A bird can also display **hormonal biting**. This occurs when a fully grown cockatiel feels frustrated because they're unable to breed. The frustrated feelings can make the bird nippy.

When growing cockatiels are reaching the adult age of 18 months, these creatures may be more prone to biting and may not crave cuddling as often as they used to. Don't worry as this hormonal and cranky phase is normal and usually temporary.

Think of cockatiels around the age of 18 months as human teenagers craving independence. Just like any other creature, cockatiels grow up and can't remain baby cockatiels forever. The hormonal changes taking place in your pet's body can lead it to experience mood swings. Cockatiels going through this phase can act gentle and affectionate one minute, only to lunge and bite at the smallest provocation soon afterwards. Don't take this personally. Your pet can't control its hormonal changes any more than you can.

An inability to breed may cause your bird to feel frustrated and bite. The majority of hormonal changes in cockatiels takes place around spring and summer seasons. The added daylight hours signal breeding to these creatures. When it comes to hormonal biting, remember it's generally temporary and you need to be patient, allowing your bird to go through its natural course of growing up. This type of biting tends to correct itself.

Note:

- If your cockatiel's age is around 18 months and its hormonal biting is becoming more vicious, decreasing the bird's exposure to daylight during the spring and summer months may be necessary. Cover your pet's cage for about four extra hours every night for a period of two weeks.

- It's also possible to aggravate hormonal changes as a cockatiel pet owner. Doing so can trigger more biting episodes. Stay away from petting a cockatiel in the spot beneath its wings and also avoid petting the bird's back. A cockatiel's testicles or ovaries are found close to these areas. Petting these spots can stimulate the release of hormones.

- Having a mirror in your cockatiel's cage is generally not recommended. A mirror may lead to hormonal mood swings and biting. Cockatiels assume that the bird they see in the mirror is another creature. When they sing, preen and display their feathers in front of the mirror, they may feel frustrated that the "other cockatiel" isn't responding in kind. Furthermore, these birds tend to feel highly possessive of their image in the mirror, thinking the image is their mate. They may bite humans in an effort to defend their "partner" reflected back by a mirror.

- If you suspect your bird is biting because of hormonal changes, keep away from using bird beds or sleeping tents. Don't let your pet spend time in small, cozy and dark spots such as bureau drawers or cabinets. These comfortable little locations will appear like ideal nesting sites for your bird, further stimulating the release of breeding hormones that lead to biting.

Control biting, on the other hand, takes place after the bird delivers a few bites and discovers how the behavior gets the cockatiel whatever it desires. Allowing your bird to make a habit out of biting by giving in to its demands—such as handing the yummy treat after your cockatiel nips you, no matter how gently-- encourages your bird to exhibit future biting. Your reaction to your pet's bite tells it how it can achieve control of you by biting.

When you respond to your cockatiel's bites with any kind of reaction, the bird will think of your reaction as a form of reward. Whether a soft bite causes you to hand your pet food, or a particularly painful nip leads you to pull away, all these reactions tell the cockatiel biting gets work done. Even saying "ouch", tossing the bird to the side or shaking your hand reinforces in the cockatiel's mind how biting is effective because it elicits a reaction.

Just like us humans, cockatiels have moods. A cranky bird that's over stimulated or exhausted is more prone to biting. Even a generally gentle bird can bite if it's irritated or experiencing fatigue. Make sure your pet gets 10 to 12 hours of sleep each night.

Any pet that's not eating well or resting properly is bound to act grouchy and may exhibit aggressive behaviors. Don't provoke your bird by bothering it when it's busy playing, eating or sleeping. If your bird shows you it wants to be alone through signs like hissing, lunging or turning its back towards you, give it space. Sometimes all your pet may need is some alone time.

There are no shortcuts or miracle formulas when it comes to taming a pet bird that bites. You will have to dedicate time and patience if you want to earn your cockatiel's trust. This is why it's advisable you take your time in selecting the cockatiel to bring home and add to your family, especially if you have children and other pets.

Interact with a cockatiel at the pet shop or when meeting a breeder. Does the bird appear fearful and ready to bite, or does it have a lovely confidence and a gentle nature when you interact with it? Each bird is different so never select a cockatiel based on physical appearances alone.

Dealing with Biting Behavior

In cases where your new pet reacts to your attempts at bonding by biting, knowing why your cockatiel bites is very important. Find out what causes the behavior and learn how to read your cockatiel's body language.

Observe your cockatiel to decipher its body language. These birds typically give a warning sign before it delivers a bite. Look out when your pet exhibits tail fanning, hissing and eye pinning. Other things a cockatiel might do when it is about to nip is backing away into a corner, moving away from you or your hand, turning its back towards you, swaying from side to side, lifting one foot, puffing its body out to give itself a bigger appearance, moving its wings away from its body and lunging forward with its beak wide open.

When a cockatiel lunges, it's telling you to stay away or back off. As soon as your bird lunges, stop whatever activity might be provoking your pet. Allow it time to calm down and de-stress. Never force your cockatiel to do your bidding until it is acting more relaxed and less aggressive. By continuing to provoke any animal, you're creating a highly tense and confrontational environment.

When it comes to taming your cockatiel, it helps plenty to reinforce positive behavior. Give your bird praises, treats and other rewards. When your bird is exhibiting undesirable behavior, try to ignore it as much as possible and make an effort not to react physically when it bites. Don't pull your hand away, shout, push your bird aside or shake your hand in the event that your cockatiel bites. You may say a firm "no" to show your feathery friend biting or any undesirable behavior is not allowed, but do no more than that.

Ways to Earn Your Cockatiel's Trust

Now that you've learned about a cockatiel's bite—what causes most biting episodes and how not to provoke your pet—it's time to learn about earning the bird's trust. In the process of bonding with the cockatiel and getting to know one another, there could very well be occasions when your pet isn't in the best of moods. Your knowledge of biting will help you act the right way, allowing you to approach bonding experiences with less frustrations and other negative emotions.

Identifying Affection

Whenever your cockatiel is craving affection from you, it will typically bend its head in a submissive manner. Even though you might be tempted to begin petting the back of your pet's neck immediately, do take it slow. Select a cue word or sound (like a soft, loving kissing sound) so your bird will eventually associate your chosen verbal cue with affection. A vocal cockatiel may even try to copy the sound you make.

Approach your pet from the front. Never sneak up behind a cockatiel. This makes them feel insecure since they love to know what's going on in their environment. Next, steadily and slowly move an index finger towards the cockatiel. Curl the other fingers in your moving hand around the thumb. You may now gently scratch your pet.

Softly stroke a cockatiel's head, beginning at the beak and moving towards the tips of the bird's crest feathers. Each cockatiel will have its own personal petting preference. Some birds love having their crest feathers' tips softly and gently twirled. Use your index finger and thumb to do the gentle twisting. Have the tips between these two fingers. Some birds love having their necks or heads stroked while some do not. Respect your pet's personal preferences.

During petting sessions, the bird might get tired or bored. If your cockatiel begins to get nippy or act stressed in any way, ignore it and leave it alone for a few hours. You want your pet to think of your bonding moments in a positive light. Don't force a cockatiel to give or receive affection when its mood dictates otherwise.

Once a cockatiel determines you're not a threat who will hurt it, and that your presence provides pleasant experiences, your pet will all the more love being around you and offer you affection in return.

Helping a Cockatiel Cope with Fear

Cockatiels are happiest when housed in a secure environment. A bird who feels safe will be more affectionate, gentle and great company. These animals feel the most secure when they live in enclosures or cages that are designed with corners. Keep away from dome-shaped or round cages.

Here are some tips to provide your cockatiel with the most secure type of dwelling:

- Placing your bird's cage up against a wall and far away from openings like doors, windows or hallways will enhance its feelings of security. Spots where the cockatiel can't observe people, other pets or vehicles approaching aren't recommended. These pets love to

83

know what's going on around them and they're smart enough to take notice.

- Whether you're taking your bird home for the first time or you've had it for a while, always maintain low to moderate noise and activity levels at home. A quiet and predictable household appeals to cockatiels.

- Don't allow other pets, especially dogs and cats, near the bird cage. If there are small pet rodents at home, house them in another room.

- If you don't live alone, encourage the rest of your family to regularly interact with the cockatiel. It can be as simple as singing the bird a song. Even family members who aren't particularly fond of petting animals can bond with a cockatiel by talking to the creature in a gentle tone.

- When placing new objects like brand new toys inside the cockatiel's cage, or when housing your bird inside a new enclosure, start by leaving out the new items or cage next to your pet. Leave the items out for a few days. Allow the cockatiel to get used to these new objects. Don't just grab a cockatiel, place it in a new cage and expect the bird to feel relaxed.

- To bond quicker while lessening your pet's fears towards new food, prepare some of the same food for yourself as well. Offer the food while partaking along with the cockatiel.

- Whenever your pet suddenly begins to bite or act grumpy outside its cage, return the bird back into the cage for a quick "timeout". Don't bother the cockatiel until it appears significantly calmer.

While we all strive to provide a stress-free environment free of sudden changes to our pets, real life requires all creatures to adapt to changes to some degree. Help your bird handle changes better by exposing it to a wide array of situations and places while the pet is young.

For example, when you have visitors over, ask them to talk to a young cockatiel. Take your pet on a tour around your home, visiting various rooms and even places outside once the cockatiel's wings have been clipped (See the next chapter to learn more about clipping your pet's wings).

You can even bring a cockatiel with you when picking up the children from school or when visiting friends. The key is to do these activities as early as possible, while the cockatiel is young.

85

Bonding with a Cage-Bound Cockatiel

When a cockatiel spends all of its time inside a cage, it becomes what's known as a cage-bound bird. Cockatiels that don't get enough time outside their cages and are lacking bonding time with humans become extra attached to their dwelling places. These birds are more fearful than cockatiels that spend a healthy amount of time outside its enclosure.

When you constantly ignore your pet cockatiel and leave it alone at home all day, it will get used to the solitary life on one hand, while feeling stressed on the other. A bored cockatiel will sometimes try to pick at its own feather while a fearful cage-bound one is more prone to biting.

Cockatiels that have been rescued from neglectful or abusive owners, or those kept in a cage at a pet shop for too long, act highly territorial and possessive of their toys, cages and food. They tend to act neurotic and feel only secure when they're safe inside their cage.

If you happen to have a pet cockatiel that's too attached to its cage, you will need to gently coax it out. Plenty of patience from your end is required. Begin by talking to the bird every day. Read it poetry or sing songs around its cage. When you see the cockatiel acting less stressed around you, only then should you begin to physically handle it. Never grab it suddenly. Leave the cage door open and have a treat in hand. Wait for a cage-bound bird to approach you and always, always let it decide to trust you on its own time and terms.

Training Your Cockatiel

Step Up Command

The "step up" command is the most popular and useful trick to teach your cockatiel. When your pet has been comfortable eating out of your hand, it typically will step onto your hand naturally. You won't have to do anything to get the cockatiel to do this, except earn its trust of course. But even if your pet already hops onto your hand on its own, you should teach it a "step up" cue.

If your pet tends to bite, move your hand or finger in a slow and steady way. Avoid quick and sudden movements. Move your finger or hand slowly towards the cockatiel's lower body, right above the bird's legs. Think of your pet's upper legs as invisible, imagine moving your hand directly through air. The motion you're aiming for here is pretty much how you would move a hand through a candle flame.

Avoid pulling your hand back as this will give a nippy cockatiel the chance to bite. Remember, most birds don't like sudden movements. The goal is to move your hand faster than what your cockatiel can see. When your pet steps up to your hand or finger, offer a treat you know it loves and say a verbal praise.

In case your cockatiel is not positively responding to this method and is beginning to act aggressive or aloof, stop to try the following day. Give yourself and your bird a break. Promoting a situation that your bird perceives to be a confrontational experience may lead it to bite or flee.

Another way to get your cockatiel to "step up" is by moving your hand slowly towards the top portion of your pet's legs, on the spot located below its abdomen. Then, apply soft pressure to the top portion of the cockatiel's legs, using a slightly upward motion towards the bird's body. Doing so will motivate your bird to step up onto your palm or fingers. As soon as it does, offer a reward immediately while delivering a verbal praise. Always use an affectionate and gentle tone.

Using Cue Words

When teaching your cockatiel to step up on command, you'll need a cue word. It can be "step up" or "jump". Say the cue word as you move your hand towards the bird, completing the hand motions described above.

Cockatiels are smart enough to associate words with specific actions or things. Using a cue word tells your pet precisely why you have a hand moving towards it. Your bird will also eventually learn to associate food rewards and verbal praises with the cue word, provided the pet accomplishes the task you are requesting.

In cases where the cockatiel exhibits aggressive behavior during training, make an effort to ignore it. You may say "no" but don't do more than that. These creatures don't react to negative reinforcement and giving your cockatiel a small shove or yelling at it will only teach it to lose trust in you. As soon as your bird starts acting grouchy or nippy, stop training to avoid creating a tense situation. Remind your cockatiel that you love it and continue your training sessions the following day.

When you soon find your cockatiel getting out of its cage and approaching you willingly, always offer verbal praise and treats right away. Most cockatiels will require a few days of practice and training before they step up on command. The more negative experiences a bird has, the later in time this will happen. Adjust your patience levels and efforts based on your pet's temperament.

Training Tips:

- It helps to train and practice in neutral locations. Find a room away from your cockatiel's cage. You may use a chair and have your pet step up from the back portion of the chair, then onto your open palm, and back to the chair again.

- Don't let training sessions drag on. Keep them for about five to ten minutes long in duration. It's best to engage your cockatiel in several short training sessions throughout each day, rather than attempt to train it for over 10 minutes. By repeating commands too much in one session, the cockatiel can get bored and associate training with a negative thought.

- Taking your bird out of the cage a few times each day to train will give the cockatiel more opportunities to socialize and get used to your presence.

- During training sessions, bring your cockatiel back to its cage while your pet is still in a calm mood. Don't wait for your pet to get tired before returning it to the security of the cage. Make sure to leave your pet's previous experience outside of the cage as a positive one.

Stick Taming

Some cockatiels will respond to the "step up" command when a perch or ladder is involved. Instead of stepping onto your fingers or palm, have your pet step up onto a perch or ladder. Move the object in pretty much the same way you would your palm.

This method is known as "stick taming" or "stick training" and it's a great alternative method for cockatiels that are afraid of human hands. If you're dealing with a cage-bound pet, have its wings trimmed and leave the door of its cage wide open. Make sure there are toys and a bowl of fresh food on top of the cage. Soon the cockatiel will venture out of the cage by itself. As soon as you observe your pet do this, offer verbal praise and reward your pet with its favorite food.

From the top of the cage where the food is located, you may then begin to teach the cockatiel the "step up". Practice this for several days.

Returning Home

When returning your feathery companion back to its cage, have the cockatiel perch on top of your hand when possible. Make sure your pet is facing you and have your hand right next to your chest or waist. Doing so blocks the cockatiel's view of any escape routes.

When you've reached the bird cage, place your hand close to the front perch. Allow the cockatiel to step back on its own. Say a cue word like "home" whenever you bring the bird back to its enclosure. Never fail to offer verbal praises as soon as your cockatiel steps on the porch. Hand your bird a treat right away. Soon it will associate the cue word "home" with its safe return to the cage.

If your cockatiel keeps on flying away from you, you will need to have its wings trimmed. The following chapter will cover wing-trimming and other grooming tips to keep your lovable cockatiel close to you, healthy and happy.

93

Chapter 4: Health and Wellness

Cockatiels are some of the most charming and lovable birds you can have as a pet. Aside from being very sociable, these feathery companions are adorable and relatively clean. With the proper care, your cockatiel will have a long and happy life, adding brightness to any bird-loving home.

These birds make excellent companions, but they need to be kept healthy and treated with respect. In this chapter you will learn how to care for your pet's health and keep it in top physical condition.

Grooming

Cockatiels require plenty of grooming. The feathers of these cute birds need care in order to keep them clean. Most of the grooming is fortunately accomplished by the bird itself. You should keep your cockatiel and its living quarters extra clean and bacteria-free by lending a helping hand, of course.

Other grooming necessities like trimming your cockatiel's feathers are as vital as the bird's hygiene routine in some cases. Failing to trim the pet's feather will make it less prone to bond and depend on you. There is, of course, the risk of your cockatiel escaping by flying away.

Read on to discover the grooming tasks you need to accomplish for a beautiful bird that enjoys your company.

Bathing Options

Giving your cockatiel the chance to bathe is crucial. When your bird gets to bathe often, you help it avoid having dry skin. The water helps in softening the keratin coating that naturally occurs on fresh feathers. Making sure your pet gets regular bathing furthermore keeps the feathers looking attractive and clean.

Cockatiels are known to produce plenty of powder down, a naturally occurring powder that appears on the bird's feathers. These creatures produce more dust than any other type of birds. Bathing will significantly cut down the presence of feather dust. It's mandatory you control the amount of dust on your cockatiel since breathing in excess dust can make your pet ill.

Here are bath tips to remember:

- Pet birds must be allowed to have as many baths as they wish. Certain birds enjoy water and having a daily bath. Some cockatiels might simply tolerate a few spray baths on a weekly basis. Each bird will have its own personal bathing preferences.

95

- It's advisable for baths to occur in the morning, giving your cockatiel lots of time to dry off its body before bedtime. A damp bird can't possibly have a comfortable night's rest.

- Keep windows near your cockatiel's bathing area closed. These pets should always be kept from drafty areas, more so while they're taking a bath.

- Your cockatiel's feathers should be allowed to dry naturally after each bath. Never use a blow dryer. Not only will its loud sound frighten most birds, a rapid change of temperature is never a good idea for cockatiels. In case your pet is soaking wet, dry it off gently with a soft terry cloth towel.

Ways to Bathe Cockatiels

These birds enjoy being sprayed with a light water mist. Spraying sessions let oils and other greasy substances run off the creature's feathers, leaving the birds clean.

One other way you can bathe your cockatiel is by using a wide, durable and shallow dish. You may use any appropriate container, one that can hold an inch of water. Fill up the container with tepid water and allow your cockatiel to roll around the water where it will most likely get the undersides of its wings wet.

You may find bird bath dishes at pet shops. Keep an eye out for bird bath dishes that come equipped with a mirror located at the bottom of the dish. The mirror is supposed to encourage your cockatiel to explore the water.

If you want to keep costs down, a simple and flat dish or pan you already own will work. The wider the dish, the more room your pet will have to enjoy baths. Place the dish or pan on a counter where you won't mind being drenched, such as a kitchen counter.

There is also the easy and fun option of giving your cockatiel a misting bath each day, from outside the cage. Pet birds that don't like using bath dishes can get clean this way with ease. Use a brand new water mist bottle. Pet shops carry them or you can find a suitable bottle at a shop that sells garden supplies. When spraying your cockatiel, spray the water facing up into air. This way the mist falls down on the cockatiel like rain, helping you avoid spraying water roughly and directly into the bird.

Some cockatiels may initially be scared of the spray bottle because of the sound the spraying creates. You can help a jittery bird adjust slowly to the bottle. Days before you give the cockatiel its very first spray bath, spray water using the bottle around the cage each day. The goal is to get your pet used to the sound coming from the spray bottle. To take it a step further, a few days before the first spray bath, you can spray your hair or hands in front of the cockatiel. This will make the bottle and the accompanying mist appear far less threatening in your pet's eyes.

Eventually your cockatiel will become so used to mist baths, it will begin to enjoy the sessions and want to get wet. You may find your bird raising its wings. This means the cockatiel wants to get the undersides of its wings wet. When this happens, mist your bird's wings on their front and back regions. After a misting bath, always empty the water out of the spray bottle and allow the bottle to fully dry. This way, bacteria won't be calling the spray bottle home.

It's not rare for cockatiels to love bathing under running water. It's real cute to see a pet bird enjoying a bath under a faucet. There are some cockatiels that enjoy their baths right next to their owners in the shower. You can find special perches available for sale, perches that mount inside the wall of a bath so pet birds can mount on them.

If you happen to be one of the lucky owners of a cockatiel who enjoys bathing with humans, ensure your pet never comes in contact with hot water or soap. Furthermore, the force of water coming directly from a shower head can be too strong to a small creature like your cockatiel. The best water flow inside the shower for these pets is water that splashes from the wall onto the cockatiel.

Nervous Bathers

There are some birds that are very jittery and nervous, anything new scares them. Even a simple task like bathing becomes a challenge when you're dealing with a stressed bird. If you have to work with such a cockatiel, don't push the bird too soon. You should approach your pet gently and encourage it to bathe until it realizes the activity can be fun and will leave them feeling good.

Whenever you notice your cockatiel try to take a bath in its water dish, place a plate of water inside your pet's cage. You may try to gently coax the bird out of its cage and offer it a spray mist bath. The sound of rain can make cockatiels crave bathing sessions. The same thing can happen thanks to the sound of running water coming from a faucet.

Each day, offer a nervous cockatiel a shallow plate filled with water. See if this helps encourage your bird to take a bath. If you want to use the spray mist method when bathing a scared bird, allow your pet to perch on your hand then hold the cockatiel over the bathroom sink. Let your pet see its image in the mirror. The bird will assume its image is another real cockatiel. Next, give the bird a few gentle mists of water.

Verbally praise your feathery pal for being good and not attempting to fly away from you. Have treats ready so you can reward your pet right after its first few bathing sessions. This will help instill in your pet's mind that bathing is a positive experience to enjoy.

Don't rush your bird into acquiring good bathing habits. Depending on the cockatiel's natural disposition, it will take as little as a few hours to even months before it accepts bathing willingly. By introducing various kinds of bathing methods to your cockatiel, you are gradually and gently teaching your pet how grooming can be fun and safe.

Trimming the Feathers

To keep your cockatiel from escaping by flying away, it's vital for its wing feathers to be trimmed. Don't worry, **if you don't feel comfortable enough doing this on your own, you can**

have a professional at a pet shop or your vet complete this task.

Like all birds, cockatiels will make an attempt to flee by flying when it's frightened. By making sure your pet's wings are trimmed, you will keep it from attempting to take flight. The good news is you can provide your bird with different levels of flight capability. The level of flight a bird has is determined by the amount of feathers clipped from the wings.

If you have a young cockatiel chick that hasn't learned how to fly, it's best to clip its wings gradually over time. Don't clip the wings of very young birds in one session. Birds that are allowed to naturally learn to fly, land and employ their own bodies to move around turn out to be more confident pets. By removing a bird's ability to take flight when it's too young, they can grow up nervous and even neurotic.

How do you clip the wings of a cockatiel that is just beginning to learn the art of flying? Clip just the two flight feathers located outside each of your pet's wing. The bird will be slowed down from this but the minimal clipping will allow it to continue to fly. A week later, follow up the task by clipping the next two feathers. Wait another week then clip another two feathers.

By following this schedule, your cockatiel will have lost its flying capabilities only when it's a grounded bird, one who has slowly but surely learned to control its movements by walking around. This should leave you with a confident bird that knows how to hop around and land, despite not having full flight capabilities.

Note: A good breeder will typically employ this clipping method before sending any of their cockatiels to its new home.

Cockatiels that have been clipped at a very young age will frequently end up with crash landings. These can break tail feathers or cause further injuries. That's why it's never advisable to clip too much at a time when your bird has yet to learn better motor skills.

When you're doing the trimming task yourself, make an effort to clip the cockatiel's wing feathers in a symmetrical fashion. Do this by trimming both wings at an equal rate. This will keep your bird looking good and give it great balance. A bad clipping job will make moving a lot more difficult for the cockatiel.

How frequently should you clip your cockatiel's feathers? When choosing how many feathers to clip off and how often, you have to factor in your pet's environment. Does your bird stay in an aviary that comes furnished with its own safety area? If yes, allowing your pet to fly is fine and the flight capabilities will help the cockatiel get plenty of necessary exercise.

If you are planning on having your cockatiel join exhibitions, keep in mind that the judges will be taking the bird's total look into consideration. Most pet owners who like to show their cockatiels at exhibitions leave the wings unclipped.

Does your bird share a home with dogs or cats? The added danger the presence of other pets provides will mean you have to allow your cockatiel a chance to escape. Only clip enough feathers that leave some degree of flying capability.

If you're one of those owners who allows pet birds to fly inside the house, then obviously you leave more wings unclipped. In this situation, the goal is to allow your bird to fly just slowly enough so it doesn't hurt itself from flying too rapidly indoors.

If your bird has opportunities to go outside, or could possibly get through an opening left ajar, it's a wise move to provide a more severe clip. The last thing you need is a missing cockatiel that flew away.

Clipping may also help tame and calm down a territorial or bossy alpha male cockatiel. Giving him a pretty severe wing clipping can humble him down several notches. When you're starting to bond with a new adult cockatiel, it's also a smart move to give it a severe clipping. A severely clipped wing will make it easier to bond with a fully grown cockatiel since the lack of flight capabilities will make the bird more dependent on you, especially when your pet needs help moving around. In cases where you need to chase the bird, it won't have the chance to go far off and hurt itself.

Which feathers should you clip? Never clip beyond the 10 primary feathers found on your cockatiel's wings. If you would prefer to leave your pet with some flight abilities, clip fewer feathers. It is possible to clip the "secondary" feathers located farther down, thereby shortening them instead, though I don't recommend it.

It's important for cockatiels to receive wing exercises, especially if you decide to clip its feathers. Dedicate some time each day holding your pet's feet to get it to flap its wings. This way you're providing the cockatiel the opportunity to develop strong muscles in its chest since it's using whatever wing feathers are available.

Keep in mind it's never possible to fully ground cockatiels. These birds can get around well enough even with clipped wings. Even in birds whose ten primary flight feathers have been clipped from each of its wings, it's not a wise move to bring them outside while perched on your shoulder. Anything can trigger fear in birds. It can be the sound of a fast vehicle driving by your street or the noises of a wild animal outdoors. Once the cockatiel gets scared, it can suddenly take flight and risk injuring itself. If you insist on bringing your pet bird outside to get some sun or for whatever reason, bring your cockatiel out in a pet carrying cage.

When clipping your cockatiel's wing feathers, do so one at a time. Always decide how many feathers to clip beforehand. You should also determine the level of flight capabilities that matches your bird's environment.

Prior to trimming each wing feather, look at it closely. You will need to figure out whether it's a blood feather or not. Never clip blood feathers since clipping these will cause bleeding to occur. A blood feather has a feathered out tip but its base contains blood vessels and nerves. These blood feathers siphon blood and clipping at this level will cause injury and pain to your cockatiel.

If you do happen to accidentally clip a blood feather and bleeding ensues, sometimes the only method to stop the blood flow is pulling out the shaft. You can ask a vet to do this task. In pulling out the shaft of the injured blood feather, you

105

need to place a firm grasp on the shaft and pull it quickly while supporting the bird's wing bones. Seek professional assistance whenever possible.

As you're clipping feathers, never leave long stray feathers. The feathers of cockatiels are naturally meant to grow together. Each feather supports another as it grows in. Leaving a long feather right at the tip of a wing leaves your bird with the chance of getting its feathers caught or entangled. By not clipping long stray feathers in the bird's wings, there is a higher chance of accidents or injuries occurring.

How to clip cockatiel wings

Do not cut this area

Primary Feathers

Secondary Feathers

Breeding Cockatiels: Is It a Wise Choice?

For pet owners who work full-time, breeding is definitely discouraged. While cockatiel chicks are absolutely adorable, like human newborn babies, they are also absolutely helpless and dependent right after they hatch.

Cockatiel chicks greet the world naked and their eyes are completely closed. These newborns are utterly dependent on parent cockatiels for food, warmth and survival.

Bear in mind that the life of a cockatiel chick is your responsibility, should you decide to become a breeder. You also have the task of caring for the cockatiel parents, including looking at their progress after the fertilized eggs have hatched. You'll need to monitor the health of mother and father cockatiels.

It's not rare for parent and baby cockatiels to experience health issues that will require the services of an avian vet. If budget restrictions keep you from being able to afford a vet's services, it's best not to even think about breeding any kind of bird. It would be irresponsible to commit to breeding without having enough resources to cover veterinary expenses.

Choosing Cockatiels for Breeding

If you're able to breed responsibly and feel inclined to do so, it's vital to select healthy fully grown cockatiels that are not related to one another. You may request for a pre-breeding health test on breeding pairs, one performed by an avian vet. He may include both gram stains and blood tests. The tests will help determine if the cockatiels come with sub-clinical infections or deficiencies in nutrition.

You will also have to factor in the age of the birds. Don't breed cockatiels younger than 18 months old. Even though young birds may be able to perform the mating act, young cockatiel males can be infertile and possibly injure the young female birds through health issues like egg binding. Furthermore, choosing cockatiel parents that are too young takes away nutrients these growing pets need. The chicks born of parents that are not ready to breed are typically weaker than the offspring produced by fully grown cockatiels.

It's never a good idea to breed birds that are related to one another. Doing so leads to chicks born with birth defects and a myriad of other potential health problems. It's not uncommon for cockatiels born from related parents to have physical abnormalities such as deformed beaks. They may even be born with missing body parts. Other issues that can arise are deformed or missing wings, toes or legs; orthopedic health problems that will negatively affect the cockatiel's ability to fly, climb, perch or walk; malfunctioning organs; and infertility. Inbreeding can also lead to decreased egg-production, infertile eggs or a lower rate of eggs that hatch.

Choose to breed only fully grown and healthy cockatiels that come from different bloodlines.

When to Breed Cockatiels

In the wild, the natural breeding time for cockatiels occurs during the spring to early autumn months. Breeding conditions are at their finest during these seasons, thanks to warmer weather, an increased in the number of daylight hours per day, and also an increase in the amount of food and rainfall available.

When breeding birds in captivity, it helps to know how they mate in the wild so you can replicate the ideal environment. By providing extra light to your cockatiels, along with more baths or misting sessions, a nutritious diet that comes with breeder's pellets, and the availability of a cockatiel nesting box, you are encouraging the birds to breed.

Cockatiels are known to be busy breeders. They tend to breed even in captivity anytime of the year, as long as they're allowed to do so. Even though indoor environments are great for breeding, the extended exposure to artificial lighting and steady supply of food and water, plus allowing your birds breed all year, are all factors that can damage the cockatiels' health.

As a breeder, you should make sure each breeding pair experiences no more than two "births" per year. Cockatiels require rest during the other times of the year. Give your birds time to get strong and ready for the following breeding season.

Breeding can be physically and psychologically taxing on birds. Like all types of stress, this can severely and negatively affect your cockatiels' immune systems. When excessive egg-laying is involved, the female cockatiel will experience a depletion of calcium and many other nutrients. The female bird that is lacking calcium due to the excessive laying of eggs can experience health hazards like egg-binding, seizures and even sudden death.

Always take it seriously and to heart how continuous breeding throughout the year puts a massive amount of strain on any female cockatiel's reproductive system. It's your responsibility to keep cockatiels from breeding too much. Fully grown and healthy birds that have been allowed to rest following a breeding season should be the only birds allowed to breed.

Laying of the Eggs

Female cockatiel lay eggs seven to ten days after a successful mating session. It's normal for the females to lay an egg every 48 hours. A group of cockatiel eggs laid at once is called a "clutch". Clutches usually come in two to eight eggs.

Prior to your cockatiel laying an egg and while it's laying, the bird will emit extra large and smelly droppings. Don't worry as this is completely normal. There are also cases when parent cockatiels will wait until two or three eggs are laid before they begin nesting. The reason the birds wait for a bit is so that the majority of the eggs will hatch at about the same time. Eggs only begin to incubate after the parents nest on them, getting the eggs warm. Cockatiel eggs stay viable for up to a week before nesting is essential. If your parent cockatiels hesitate to enter a nesting box, it may help to hang a strip of millet seed close to the entrance of the nesting box.

Expect the cockatiel eggs to hatch 18 to 21 days after the parents begin to nest. A few days prior to hatching, there is an air cell found at the wider end of each egg that will increase in size and begin to tilt. The chick will then move about, moving the air cell in the process. This step is known as "drawdown".

When the chick is located inside the air cell, it will begin to breathe using its lungs. The baby will increasingly act more active, using up the oxygen found inside the cell. As the carbon dioxide levels rise, the chick's neck and abdominal muscles will start to contract. These contractions will then push the baby bird's back against its shell, leading the chick's feet to push against the opposite end of the shell. Thanks to the muscle contractions in the neck area of the bird, the "egg tooth" found inside the baby's beak will begin to puncture and break the inner shell.

Keep an eye out for the initial visible sign of hatching: the external pip mark. It will look like a tiny dent or bump that comes with small cracks found on the external side of the shell. This mark will grow in size as the chick breaks off the shell. When the shell is punctured and the cockatiel chick begins to breathe the air outside, you might hear some vocalization.

Newborn Cockatiels

Make sure you visually observe each chick as soon as it has hatched. A healthy baby cockatiel should have yellow-pink skin and the bird should feel warm.

When a chick is dehydrated, it will appear wrinkled and skinny. Their skin will look dry and red or muddy in color, while the skin will feel sticky when touched. Always take dehydration in your pets seriously. Dehydration is a very serious problem when it occurs in newly hatched chicks. If a baby cockatiel comes out dehydrated, give it a drop of warm Pedialyte. Do not repeat the process unless you observe the liquid go through the baby's beak and the bird has passed at least one dropping.

Some professional breeders will regularly provide baby cockatiels a drop of warm Pedialyte as soon as the birds hatch. This is to avoid dehydration. Once a normal dropping has passed, the drops are given every hour.

By instinct, cockatiel parents will take away pieces of egg shell from their chicks right after they hatch. As soon as they're done, the chick should look fluffy and clean.

Remove the empty egg shells from the nesting box as soon as you can. Failure to do so can lead to bacterial growth. Cockatiel parents might wait up to eight hours before feeding their chicks for the first time. They usually wait to allow the babies to dry.

Nature will provide nutrition to the chicks via the yolk sac. This sac is absorbed before the hatching gets completed.

Common Health Problems

The majority of health problems experienced by cockatiels are caused by malnutrition or improper care. Some health conditions are life-threatening and can swiftly end the precious life of your pet. These potentially fatal problems include Polyoma, Psittacosis, Candidiasis and Pacheco's disease.

Psittacosis

Psittacosis is known by other names such as "parrot fever" and chlamydiosis. This health condition is caused by a certain type of bacteria that is transmitted through bird droppings, feather dust and nasal secretions.

Infected cockatiels may exhibit symptoms like a runny nose, shortness of breath, lethargy, dehydration, loss of appetite or eye discharge. Consult a vet if you notice these symptoms are present in your pet for longer than a few days. Treating Psittacosis typically involves giving your bird antibiotics for about six weeks. Calcium must be removed or limited in your pet's diet.

Polyoma

Polyoma is a health problem that is caused by a virus. The viral infection generally affects younger cockatiels and transmission of the virus occurs through droppings, feather dust and respiratory secretions. The virus may furthermore be transmitted via eggs. You can have your cockatiel vaccinated against the virus that causes Polyoma. As soon as your pet reaches 40 days old, you can have a vet administer the vaccine.

Pacheco's Disease

Pacheco's disease is from a highly lethal virus. Birds that have this disease are known to experience sudden death. Symptoms of this condition include ruffled feathers, anorexia, intermittent diarrhea and lethargy. Pacheco's disease may be prevented via vaccination. Keep in mind it's possible for a bird to experience an adverse reaction to the vaccine.

Candidiasis

One of the most common health problems for cockatiels is Candidiasis. This is caused by yeast and typically affects younger cockatiel due to their underdeveloped immune systems. Adult birds with compromised immune systems can also develop this disease. Long-term use of antibiotics is believed to cause Candidiasis. When hand-feeding cockatiel chicks, make sure your hand and any equipment are sterilized to avoid spreading this condition.

Symptoms include vomiting, depression, diarrhea and weight loss. If your cockatiel's mouth or beak is infested with the yeast that causes Candidiasis, your pet may have bad breath and you might observe white material coming from its mouth. The way to treat this condition is through antifungal medications. If you suspect your pet has Candidiasis, take it to a vet immediately. Don't feed your cockatiel fruit or anything that contains sugar until the disease is treated and your pet has fully recovered.

When to See an Avian Vet

Every minor symptom your bird exhibits doesn't require a costly visit to the vet. There are certain signs to watch out for, however, that signal a bigger problem than a bad mood.

Consult an avian vet when you notice these symptoms in your cockatiel:

- Loss of appetite lasting more than a couple of days

- An untidy appearance despite proper grooming habits

- Excessive feather plucking

- Abnormal droppings

- Disorientation

- Excessive drinking

- Odd sleep behavior

- Change in normal activities like playing, talking or bonding with humans

- Changes in energy levels

- Soiled tail, wings or bottom

Tip: Making it a habit to check your pet's appearance and behavior every day will help you greatly in being aware when something is wrong. You'll be able to spot changes in your bird's behavior early on, before problems escalate.

Common Household Hazards

Never leave your cockatiel alone when it's out of the cage. These birds' playful and inquisitive nature opens them to all kinds of accidents. Losing a pet because of a household accident that could have been fully avoided with common sense and responsible pet-ownership is a truly sad experience.

It's vital to bird-proof your home and be on the lookout for any potentially harmful situations your bird may experience. Think of your cockatiel as a toddler with wings. Watch out for these common health hazards:

- Non-Stick Cookware. The American Veterinary Medical Association, along with the American Association of Poison Control Centers, report that fumes coming from overheated non-stick cookware are poisonous to birds. The toxicity is more likely to happen when these pots are left on a hot surface, causing the cookware to

119

overheat. The fumes emitting release toxic particles in the air. These particles, once inhaled, can cause irreversible damage to your cockatiel's lungs.

Note: Why are birds so sensitive to toxin in the air? Unlike many other animals, birds lack the capacity to clear toxic matter from their lungs. They're not able to exhale or cough out toxic particles. Death caused by poisonous air in birds can happen within a few seconds or a full day. When birds die from overheated non-stick cookware, they experience a very painful end.

- Chemical fumes emitted by pesticides, mothballs, perfumes, hairsprays, polish remover, ammonia, bleach, varnish, paint, paint remover, nicotine, permanent markers, air freshener (all kinds), carpet fresheners, incense, scented candles or basically any product that emits fumes have the potential to cause any bird to fall ill. Avoid using anything that releases chemical fumes at home. Completely avoid the use of pesticides around birds.

- Nicotine can be absorbed through your cockatiel's skin. If you smoke or come in contact with nicotine in any way, wash your hands before handling your pet.

- Make sure you properly store grains and seeds. The molds or fungi that can grow on them is toxic to birds. High humidity, warm weather and poor ventilation lead to toxic growth. Keep foods from becoming moldy. When a bird ingests moldy food, it can develop cancer or sudden lethal poisoning. Not all types of mold can be seen by the naked eye. Avoiding feeding any pet bird discolored, mushy, bruised fruits or veggies. The saying "when in doubt, throw it out" is best made into a serious motto to live by. Keep seeds in airtight containers and leave these containers in cool dry spots to avoid moldy food.

- If your cockatiel is well nourished and in great health, a draft won't kill it. Drafts, however, can cause the death of birds with compromised immune systems. As a general rule, never keep your cockatiel's cage in a drafty location. Be on the lookout for both cold and warm drafts. Hold a lit candle in the spot where you plan to place the cage. If you see the flame flickering, a draft exists and you must select another draft-free location.

- Ceiling fans and other hanging home accessories can cause severe injuries in birds or kill them instantly. If your cockatiel lands on a hanging lamp it may experience burnt feet.

- Some antiques and "Tiffany style" lamps contain lead-soldered into the material. A bird can die swiftly if it ingests anything with lead.

- Keep all bathrooms bird-safe by closing the lid on toilet bowls. A flying cockatiel can easily land and drown after a fall inside a toilet bowl. Your pet might mistake bubbles in tub or sink's water as a landing spot. Never leave a bird alone in any place where they can drown.

- Always ensure any door or window where your pet can fly though is kept closed. Don't allow your cockatiel to fly in a room that has medium to large mirrors. They can quickly fly straight into clear glass and mirrors, leading to injury.

- Peanuts in any form often contain a toxin called Aflatoxin. This can be deadly to cockatiels. The toxin is caused by a type of fungus that grows under the nut shells. Never feed your pet peanuts, Brazil nuts and any other nut that naturally grows inside a shell. Peanut butter may also contain Aflatoxin and should be avoided. Some good quality brands of peanut butter don't contain Aflatoxin but it's best to avoid the risk as there are plenty of other options that work great as bird treats.

With proper precaution and planning, your home can be a safe haven for your cockatiel. Aside from the affection and company it craves from you, your bird trusts you to provide it an environment where its jolly and endearing temperament will thrive in.

Additional Resources

For additional reading, I recommend these two internet forums:

http://talkcockatiels.com/forum.php

http://www.totallytiels.com/forum/

126

Made in the USA
Las Vegas, NV
19 January 2023

65899591R00075